Francis Frith's
Ireland

Photographic Memories

Francis Frith's
Ireland

Revised edition of original work by

Helen Livingston

FRITH
BOOK Co

Hardback edition published in 2000 by Frith Book Company Ltd

Revised paperback edition published in the United Kingdom in 2000 by
Frith Book Company Ltd

First published in the United Kingdom in 1998
by WBC Ltd

British Library Cataloguing in Publication Data

Francis Frith's Ireland
Helen Livingston
ISBN 1-85937-243-0

Frith Book Company Ltd
Frith's Barn, Teffont,
Salisbury, Wiltshire SP3 5QP
Tel: +44 (0) 1722 716 376
Email: info@frithbook.co.uk
www.frithbook.co.uk

Printed and bound in Great Britain

Front Cover: Belfast, The Corn Market 1897 40184

Contents

Francis Frith: *Victorian Pioneer*

FRANCIS FRITH, Victorian founder of the world-famous photographic archive, was a complex and multitudinous man. A devout Quaker and a highly successful Victorian businessman, he was both philosophic by nature and pioneering in outlook.

By 1855 Francis Frith had already established a wholesale grocery business in Liverpool, and sold it for the astonishing sum of £200,000, which is the equivalent today of over £15,000,000. Now a multi-millionaire, he was able to indulge his passion for travel. As a child he had pored over travel books written by early explorers, and his fancy and imagination had been stirred by family holidays to the sublime mountain regions of Wales and Scotland. 'What a land of spirit-stirring and enriching scenes and places!' he had written. He was to return to these scenes of grandeur in later years to 'recapture the thousands of vivid and tender memories', but with a different purpose. Now in his thirties, and captivated by the new science of photography, Frith set out on a series of pioneering journeys to the Nile regions that occupied him from 1856 until 1860.

Intrigue and Adventure

He took with him on his travels a specially-designed wicker carriage that acted as both dark-room and sleeping chamber. These far-flung journeys were packed with intrigue and adventure. In his life story, written when he was sixty-three, Frith tells of being held captive by bandits, and of fighting 'an awful midnight battle to the very point of surrender with a deadly pack of hungry, wild dogs'. Sporting flowing Arab costume, Frith arrived at Akaba by camel seventy years before Lawrence, where he encountered 'desert princes and rival sheikhs, blazing with jewel-hilted swords'.

During these extraordinary adventures he was assiduously exploring the desert regions bordering the Nile and patiently recording the antiquities and peoples with his camera. He was the first photographer to venture beyond the sixth cataract. Africa was still the mysterious 'Dark Continent', and Stanley and Livingstone's historic meeting was a decade into the future. The conditions for picture taking confound belief. He laboured for hours in his wicker dark-room in the sweltering heat of the desert, while the volatile chemicals fizzed dangerously in their trays. Often he was forced to work in remote tombs and caves where conditions were cooler. Back in London he exhibited his photographs and was 'rapturously cheered' by members of the Royal Society. His reputation as a photographer was made overnight. An eminent modern historian has likened their impact on the population of the time to that on our own generation of the first photographs taken on the surface of the moon.

Venture of a Life-Time

Characteristically, Frith quickly spotted the opportunity to create a new business as a specialist publisher of photographs. He lived in an era of immense and sometimes violent change. For the poor in the early part of Victoria's reign work was a drudge and the hours long, and people had precious little free time to enjoy themselves. Most had no transport other than a cart or gig at their disposal, and had not travelled far beyond the

boundaries of their own town or village. However, by the 1870s, the railways had threaded their way across the country, and Bank Holidays and half-day Saturdays had been made obligatory by Act of Parliament. All of a sudden the ordinary working man and his family were able to enjoy days out and see a little more of the world.

With characteristic business acumen, Francis Frith foresaw that these new tourists would enjoy having souvenirs to commemorate their days out. In 1860 he married Mary Ann Rosling and set out with the intention of photographing every city, town and village in Britain. For the next thirty years he travelled the country by train and by pony and trap, producing fine photographs of seaside resorts and beauty spots that were keenly bought by millions of Victorians. These prints were painstakingly pasted into family albums and pored over during the dark nights of winter, rekindling precious memories of summer excursions.

The Rise of Frith & Co

Frith's studio was soon supplying retail shops all over the country. To meet the demand he gathered about him a small team of photographers, and published the work of independent artist-photographers of the calibre of Roger Fenton and Francis Bedford. In order to gain some understanding of the scale of Frith's business one only has to look at the catalogue issued by Frith & Co in 1886: it runs to some 670 pages, listing not only many thousands of views of the British Isles but also many photographs of most European countries, and China, Japan, the USA and

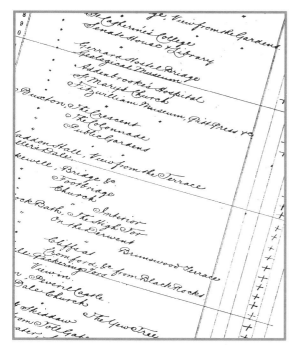

Canada – note the sample page shown above from the hand-written *Frith & Co* ledgers detailing pictures taken. By 1890 Frith had created the greatest specialist photographic publishing company in the world, with over 2,000 outlets – more than the combined number that Boots and WH Smith have today! The picture on the right shows the *Frith & Co* display board at Ingleton in the Yorkshire Dales. Beautifully constructed with mahogany frame and gilt inserts, it could display up to a dozen local scenes.

Postcard Bonanza

The ever-popular holiday postcard we know today took many years to develop. In 1870 the Post Office issued the first plain cards, with a pre-printed stamp on one face. In 1894 they allowed other publishers' cards to be sent through the mail with an attached adhesive halfpenny stamp. Demand grew rapidly, and in 1895 a new size of postcard was permitted called the court card, but there was little room for illustration. In 1899, a year after Frith's death, a new card measuring 5.5 x 3.5 inches became the standard format, but it was not until 1902 that the divided back came into being, with address and message on one face and a full-size illustration on the other. *Frith & Co* were in the vanguard of postcard development, and Frith's sons Eustace and Cyril continued their father's monumental task, expanding the number of views offered to the public and recording more and more places in Britain, as the coasts and country-side were opened up to mass travel.

Francis Frith died in 1898 at his villa in Cannes, his great project still growing. The archive he created continued in business for another seventy years. By 1970 it contained over a third of a million pictures of 7,000 cities, towns and villages. The massive photo-graphic record Frith has left to us stands as a living monument to a special and very remarkable man.

Frith's Archive: *A Unique Legacy*

FRANCIS FRITH'S legacy to us today is of immense significance and value, for the magnificent archive of evocative photographs he created provides a unique record of change in 7,000 cities, towns and villages throughout Britain over a century and more. Frith and his fellow studio photographers revisited locations many times down the years to update their views, compiling for us an enthralling and colourful pageant of British life and character.

We tend to think of Frith's sepia views of Britain as nostalgic, for most of us use them to conjure up memories of places in our own lives with which we have family associations. It often makes us forget that to Francis Frith they were records of daily life as it was actually being lived in the cities, towns and villages of his day. The Victorian age was one of great and often bewildering change for ordinary people, and though the pictures evoke an impression of slower times, life was as busy and hectic as it is today.

We are fortunate that Frith was a photographer of the people, dedicated to recording the minutiae of everyday life. For it is this sheer wealth of visual data, the painstaking chronicle of changes in dress, transport, street layouts, buildings, housing, engineering and landscape that captivates us so much today. His remarkable images offer us a powerful link with the past and with the lives of our ancestors.

Today's Technology

Computers have now made it possible for Frith's many thousands of images to be accessed almost instantly. In the Frith archive today, each photograph is carefully 'digitised' then stored on a CD Rom. Frith archivists can locate a single photograph amongst thousands within seconds. Views can be catalogued and sorted under a variety of categories of place and content to the immediate benefit of researchers.

Inexpensive reference prints can be created for them at the touch of a mouse button, and a wide range of books and other printed materials assembled and published for a wider, more general readership - in the next twelve months over a hundred Frith local history titles will be published! The day-to-day workings of the archive are very different from how they were in Francis Frith's time: imagine the herculean task of sorting through eleven tons of glass negatives as Frith had to do to locate a particular

See Frith at www. frithbook.co.uk

sequence of pictures! Yet the archive still prides itself on maintaining the same high standards of excellence laid down by Francis Frith, including the painstaking cataloguing and indexing of every view.

It is curious to reflect on how the internet now allows researchers in America and elsewhere greater instant access to the archive than Frith himself ever enjoyed. Many thousands of individual views can be called up on screen within seconds on one of the Frith internet sites, enabling people living continents away to revisit the streets of their ancestral home town, or view places in Britain where they have enjoyed holidays. Many overseas researchers welcome the chance to view special theme selections, such as transport, sports, costume and ancient monuments.

We are certain that Francis Frith would have heartily approved of these modern developments in imaging techniques, for he himself was always working at the very limits of Victorian photographic technology.

The Value of the Archive Today

Because of the benefits brought by the computer, Frith's images are increasingly studied by social historians, by researchers into genealogy and ancestory, by architects, town planners, and by teachers and schoolchildren involved in local history projects.

In addition, the archive offers every one of us an opportunity to examine the places where we and our families have lived and worked down the years. Highly successful in Frith's own era, the archive is now, a century and more on, entering a new phase of popularity.

The Past in Tune with the Future

Historians consider the Francis Frith Collection to be of prime national importance. It is the only archive of its kind remaining in private ownership and has been valued at a million pounds. However, this figure is now rapidly increasing as digital technology enables more and more people around the world to enjoy its benefits.

Francis Frith's archive is now housed in an historic timber barn in the beautiful village of Teffont in Wiltshire. Its founder would not recognize the archive office as it is today. In place of the many thousands of dusty boxes containing glass plate negatives and an all-pervading odour of photographic chemicals, there are now ranks of computer screens. He would be amazed to watch his images travelling round the world at unimaginable speeds through network and internet lines.

The archive's future is both bright and exciting. Francis Frith, with his unshakeable belief in making photographs available to the greatest number of people, would undoubtedly approve of what is being done today with his lifetime's work. His photographs, depicting our shared past, are now bringing pleasure and enlightenment to millions around the world a century and more after his death.

Belfast

The second largest city in Ireland, just over 100 miles north of Dublin, it is the capital of Northern Ireland. It is a city born of the industrial revolution, with extensive docks, ship-building and heavy industry. The centre is based around Donegall Square, including the magnificent City Hall and the Linen Hall library. Other notable buildings include both Protestant and Catholic cathedrals, and the Victorian Queen's University. South of the city are the Botanic Gardens, with an excellent curvilinear glasshouse.

Belfast, High Street 1897 40176
This view looks away from the Albert Memorial. The cobbled surface is clearly visible with the rails of the horse tram curving away sharply to the left. The large scale of many of Belfast's buildings is also apparent.

Belfast, High Street 1897 40175
Looking down the busy, bustling high street to the Albert Memorial clock tower. Horse-drawn trams vie with the carts for the road, whilst the street is busy with shoppers.

Belfast, Victoria Street 1897 40179
Another view of Belfast city, with the Albert Memorial as the focal point. This time, the photographer is in Victoria Street, looking north from near the junction with Chichester Street. Church Lane and Victoria Square are just visible to the left.

Belfast, Victoria Street 1897 40180
A fine view looking north up Victoria Street from the junction with Ann Street. The view is again dominated by the Albert Memorial. The cobbled streets are much in evidence, and the road belongs to pedestrians.

Belfast, Ann Street 1897 40188
A view looking east along Ann Street from Victoria Street. Horse-drawn trams are again in evidence. In the middle distance can be seen Queen's Bridge over the River Lagan, and beyond is industrial Belfast hard at work.

Belfast, The Corn Market 1897 40184
This is a short street just off High Street that links it to Arthur Square. The cobbled streets are seen clearly, as are the jaunting cars, carts and a bike.

Belfast, Albert Memorial 1897 40183
Perhaps the most famous landmark in Belfast, the Albert Memorial tower was built shortly after Albert's death and is 143 ft high. The statue of the Prince Consort gazes benevolently down High Street. The tower, built on reclaimed land, now leans slightly.

Belfast, Royal Avenue 1897 40185
A view looking down the avenue, with two horse-drawn trams in the foreground. At this time, although authority had been obtained to electrify the system, this did not happen until it was taken over by the corporation in 1904.

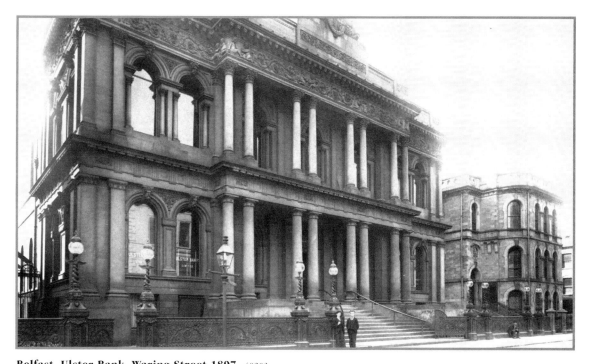

Belfast, Ulster Bank, Waring Street 1897 40203
A fine view of one of Belfast's many imposing buildings, the Ulster Bank in Waring Street. It was built in 1860 and still stands today. Italianate in style with fluted pillars, the statuary on the front is a well-known landmark.

111,148

**Belfast, Castle Place
1897** 40187A
The handsome
buildings of Belfast in
Castle Place. The Belfast
trams are again in
evidence: the gauge
was 4 ft 8 in, rather
than the Irish standard
of 5 ft 3 in. The last
tram ran in 1954, but
trolleybuses continued
until 1968.

◀ **Belfast, Botanic Gardens 1897** 40212
A splendid view of the gardens, taken when they were already seventy years old. The gardens, near Queen's University, are still a restful oasis to the south of the city. The fine Palm House stands to the left, and is a major attraction.

◄ Belfast, Queen's College 1897 40201
A view of what became Queen's University. It is situated to the south of the city centre, and was first established in 1849. It became a separate university about 10 years after this picture was taken.

▼ Belfast, The Castle 1897 40214
The castle is superbly situated a few miles to the north of the city, on Cave Hill overlooking Belfast Lough. It was built in 1870 by the Third Marquess of Donegal and was given to the city in 1934.

◄ Belfast, Stormont 1936 87696
A fine study of the Parliament buildings when they were only four years old. Stormont is situated about five miles to the east of Belfast. Built in neoclassical style, it was a gift of the Government to the people of Northern Ireland. It housed the Northern Irish Parliament until 1972.

Belfast, Isle of Man Steamer 1897 40232
A view of the steamer at Belfast Docks. There are still summer sailings from Belfast to the Isle of Man. In the background can be seen glimpses of heavy industry, Belfast being world-famous for its Harland and Woolf shipyard.

The North East

BANGOR

Bangor is a busy industrial town and seaside resort situated on Belfast Lough, at the northern end of the Ards Peninsula. It has a noble past, the site of a great sixth-century abbey, a sacred spot of the Celtic Catholic Church, which was founded by St Comgall. The abbey was sacked by the Danes and, although refounded later, was eventually dissolved by Henry VIII. The present town was founded by Sir James Hamilton for Scottish settlers in the early seventeenth century.

DONAGHADEE

A small town on the east coast of County Down, about seven miles east of Bangor. As one of the closest points to Scotland, the harbour, designed by John Rennie, was once a thriving little port with a mail service to Portpatrick on the Wigtownshire coast. It lost that business to Larne back in the mid-nineteenth century, and is today a pleasant seaside and harbour town, with an old pub once visited by Peter the Great and Keats.

Bangor, The Front 1897 40250
This view, taken from the seafront looking back to the town, shows the quieter aspect of 'Belfast by the Sea', Bangor's affectionate nickname.

GREY ABBEY

This pleasant village lies on the shores of Strangford Lough on the Ards Peninsula in County Down. It is famed for its ruinous Cistercian Abbey, founded in 1193 by Affreca, wife of John de Courcy, and dissolved in 1537. The abbey church was later re-roofed and served as the parish church until 1778.

DOWNPATRICK

The county town of Down, this pleasant market town lies about twenty-two miles southeast of Belfast, and is surrounded by countryside rich in antiquities. There is a Protestant cathedral, rebuilt on the site of a foundation stretching back to the beginning of the Celtic church. The suffix 'Patrick' celebrates the supposed discovery here of the grave of St Patrick, who may have founded the first church here.

HILLSBOROUGH

A small town in County Down founded by English settlers and still very English in atmosphere, with pleasant Georgian houses down its steep main street. It takes its name from its founder, Sir Arthur Hill, who built the fort here in the days of Charles I. This was constituted a Royal Fortress by Charles II. William III slept here on his way to the battle of the Boyne. There is notable wrought ironwork in the gates to Government House, the former residence of the Governor of Northern Ireland.

CARRICKFERGUS

An old town, it lies on the north shore of Belfast Lough between Belfast and Larne. It was once an important seaport, but is now a commuter and seaside town, best known for its castle. There are some good buildings in the town, and some of the seventeenth-century town walls can still be traced. The castle has been a stronghold ever since it was built in the thirteenth century, and even today it dominates the town and harbour. There is a plaque and statue commemorating the spot where William III landed on 14 June 1690.

WHITEHEAD

A small seaside resort in County Antrim, it is situated at the mouth of Belfast Lough about halfway between Belfast and Larne. There are some remains of Castle Chester, built in Elizabethan times. There are fine walks round the coast to Black Head and on the eastern side of Larne Lough.

LARNE

The linen manufacturing town of Larne, which lies at the southern end of the magnificent Antrim Coast Road, and close to the famous Glens of Antrim, is best known as the ferry terminus for the shortest crossing to the British

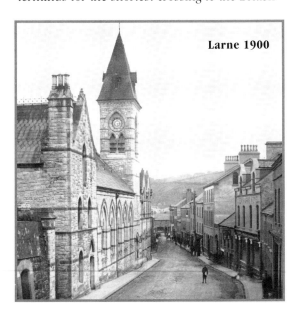

Larne 1900

Portrush 1897

mainland (Stranraer). The harbour is guarded by the Chaine memorial tower, a 95 ft-high round tower which looks ancient but is modern. The Curran, a promontory south of the town, was an important site for flint implement manufacture in Neolithic times.

GIANT'S CAUSEWAY

This superb basaltic platform, a World Heritage Site, thrusts out into the sea towards Scotland from the cliffed Antrim coast. The feature is famed for its 'pavement' of hexagonal basaltic columns formed by cooling of the molten rock at depth, though legend holds that this 'causeway' was constructed by the giant Finn MacCool who, in his fight with a Scottish giant, started to build a roadway to Scotland.

PORTRUSH

An attractive seaside resort and harbour town, Portrush is situated on the north coast of Ireland on Ramore Head, a rocky peninsula with fine views to Donegal, Rathlin Island and the Mull of Kintyre. Situated at the end of the famous Antrim Coast Road, it is close to the Giant's

Causeway, and was once linked to it by an electric tramway.

BALLYMONEY

This is a farming and linen town in the Bann valley near Coleraine. It is situated on the main road from Ballymena to Coleraine, and it also has a station on the Belfast to Londonderry railway line. It was settled by the Scots and the spacious high street and generously proportioned buildings are evidence of its prosperity.

ARDBOE

An ancient site, on the west shore of Lough Neagh, the largest lake in the British Isles. There are the ruins of a medieval church, a fine cross and an abbey founded in the sixth century. The lake was supposed to have curative properties and the site was a place of pilgrimage.

LISBURN

Now a suburb of Belfast, this town in the Lagan valley was originally colonised by English and

Welsh settlers. Then, in the late seventeenth century, Huguenot refugees started Ulster's famous linen industry here. The church, in 'Planter's Gothic', was granted Cathedral status in 1662, and there are some pleasant Georgian houses. Sir Richard Wallace (1818-90), whose widow presented London's Wallace Collection to the nation, was a native of Lisburn.

DROMORE

A cathedral and market town, situated on the Belfast to Newry road about sixteen miles south west of Belfast. A monastery was founded here in the seventh century, but the present-day cathedral dates from the seventeenth century. The earlier church was burned down in 1641.

FINTONA

This small town lies just south of Omagh in County Tyrone. It was noted for its horse-drawn tramway, built in 1883, which connected the town to the railway station, less than a mile away. It closed in 1957.

MONAGHAN

Monaghan is a rural county town that was granted a charter of incorporation by James I. There is a Catholic cathedral, the seat of the Bishop of Clogher, a town in County Tyrone, Northern Ireland. Although originally one of the nine counties of Ulster, Monaghan is one of the three counties (Donegal and Cavan are the others) which are today in Southern Ireland. The River Blackwater flows through the county, heading northeast to Lough Neagh.

LOUGHGALL

Notorious as the spot where eight IRA men were killed in an army ambush in 1988, this attractive little village in the fruit-growing district of Armagh has returned to peace and quiet with antique shops along its main street. Nearby is the little Lough Gall that christened the village. The inhabitants are strongly Protestant and it was here that the first Orange Lodge was founded in 1795, and today there is an Orange Museum.

Bangor, The Esplanade 1897

Bangor Bay 1897 40238
Another fine view of the bay, showing the town crowding down to the waterfront and the townsfolk taking a stroll.
The marina and Pickie Fun Park now occupy this part of the waterfront.

▼ **Bangor, Town View 1897** 40261
A view of part of the town from the old pier, showing to advantage
the turrets and crow-stepped gable of Sir James Hamilton's Custom
House. In the mud are various beached craft. Today, Bangor is home
to the Royal Ulster Yacht Club's annual regatta.

▼ **Bangor Bay 1897** 40237
A superb view, with a steamer just arriving at the pier. During the sixth
century, many of St Comgall's disciples set out in their coracles from a
rocky reef near the steamer pier. Many of western Europe's
monasteries were founded by these missionaries from Bangor.

▲ **Bangor, The Esplanade
1897** 40253
Bangor is a bustling
commuter and seaside
town, conveniently
situated about thirteen
miles from Belfast. This
bustling view shows the
bandstand on the left and
the 'Scottish baronial
style' Old Custom House
of 1637 in the middle
distance.

◀ **Bangor 1897** 40241
A busy scene of Bangor,
showing the piers and
sailing boats. In addition to
the pedestrians, the main
traffic is typical Irish jaunting
cars and wagons. A solitary
lady can be seen on her
bike.

Bangor, Bowman's Terrace 1897 40259
Taken nearer to the town, this view shows the strong Scottish influence in much of Bangor's architecture. Two girls in pinafores watch the passers-by from the bench in the foreground.

Bangor, Bathing Place 1897 40264
A view looking out over Belfast Lough. A crowd of people watch the bathers. Note the lady with a parasol. To the right of the picture, there is a swimmer on the diving platform.

Bangor, Main Street 1897 40267
This view, taken from the bottom of Main Street, looks up the hill towards the station. It shows the bustling town, with a carriage and a cart the only wheeled traffic.

Belfast, View of Cave Hill 1897 40217
Belfast is pleasantly situated at the end of the lough that bears its name. This view looks westwards across the lough to Cave Hill, just to the north of the city. The castle is visible part way up the hill. Beneath the castle, the outer suburbs stretch along the shore of the lough.

Donaghadee, The Seafront 1897 40287
This close-up of the seafront shows the Imperial Hotel, while in the distance is the restored parish church, with a Jacobean tower, dating from 1641.

◄ **Donaghadee, The Wharf 1897** *40286*
Another view of the charming seaside town and port, this time looking to the prominent landmark, the 70 ft mound and ruined castle of 1821.

◄ Donaghadee 1897
40285

A view looking south round the sweep of the bay to the little harbour, once used by the mail boats to Portpatrick in Wigtownshire. Boats are drawn up on the pebbled beach, where girls are playing.

▼ Grey Abbey c1955
G269002

An evocative view of this pleasant town which takes its name from the ruinous Cistercian Abbey.

◄ Grey Abbey c.1955
G269001

A view showing roads virtually devoid of traffic. Grey Abbey was once the post town on the Newtownards to Portaferry road.

Downpatrick, Irish Street c1900 D76002
A view of one of the three main streets in the little town, the others being English Street and Scottish Street. The town has some interesting Georgian buildings and a tenth-century cross outside the cathedral.

Hillsborough, The Courthouse c1890 H142005
Originally built in 1760 as a market house, the courthouse, which stands in the centre of the square, was enlarged in 1810.

Hillsborough, Main Street c1890 H142006
An evocative view showing, on the right, the statue of the fourth Marquess of Downshire. The conductor Sir Hamilton Harty was born in Hillsborough, where his father was church organist.

Hillsborough Castle, The Gatehouse 1890 H14203
The gatehouse is a little fort in the Gothic style, converted in 1770, with Gothic pointed doors and windows.

▼ **Hillsborough, Courthouse Square and Main Street 1890** H14202
There are fine Georgian buildings, both in the square and down the
steep slope, making Hillsborough one of the most attractive towns in
Northern Ireland.

▼ **Carrickfergus Castle 1897** 40275
A fine study taken from the pier, showing the vast bulk of the castle
towering above the little seaside town which has grown up in its
shadow.

▲ **Carrickfergus Castle,
1897** 40276
A close-up view of the
castle, which was built in
Norman times and was in
continuous use until this
century. Note the superb
lines of the yacht to the
right of the picture.

◀ **Carrickfergus, The Coast Road 1898** 40282
A view looking north along the coast road with the castle behind the photographer. This charming scene has captured women and children out walking, with not a wheeled vehicle to be seen.

Carrickfergus, View from the Quay c1897 40280
A view looking down Belfast Lough to Carrickfergus and the harbour. The town and church can be seen inland of the castle, ranged beneath the slopes of Knockagh. A ship lies rotting by the quay.

Carrickfergus, View from the Quay c1897 40281
Another view from the quay, which is situated just to the north of Carrickfergus. It shows the little harbour wall and a rather full rowing boat setting out on an excursion.

Whitehead, The Beach 1897 40292
Whitehead is a popular resort and the pebble beach is much in evidence in this view looking round to Black Head.
A little girl is playing among the rocks. Note the refreshment room behind the hotel.

Whitehead, The Beach 1897 40295
Another view, this time looking south along the beach towards Carrickfergus. Belfast Lough is on the left, and the
hotel and refreshment room are on the right.

**Larne, Main Street
1900** L142012
An excellent view of
Boyd's souvenir shop,
situated in Larne's Main
Street. A wide range of
knick-knacks of all
descriptions are waiting
for customers. One of
the hoardings above the
window advertises the
renowned Irish Linen.

**Larne, Main Street
c1890** L142001
A party of three
carriages of sightseers
await to depart from
Larne Main Street.
Larne is the start of the
famous Antrim Coast
Road to Portrush,
perhaps the most
spectacular coast
journey in the British
Isles. It was popular
even in Victorian times.

◀ **Larne 1900** L142011
This view emphasises
the rather stern aspect
of the town. Its major
attraction is the
Oldersfleet Castle ruins,
near Curran Point and
the harbour.

Larne, Glynn c1890

L142002

A charming view of Glynn, a little Irish village about a mile to the south of Larne, on the western edge of Larne Lough. Just to the south of the village are the ruins of the old church.

Larne, View from Promenade 1900

L142010

This view shows the entrance to the harbour dominated by the 95 ft-high Chaine memorial tower, a nineteenth-century reproduction of a round tower. Opposite is Island Magee (not really an island but a long peninsula), which is connected to Larne by a ferry.

Giant's Causeway, The Wishing Arch c1897

40421

The character of Antrim's coast is nowhere better expressed than where it is possible to see the black basalt overlying the white chalk rocks, as here at the Wishing Arch.

View from Giant's Causeway 1897 40423
Looking back to Aird Snout, the hexagonal structure of the Giant's Causeway can be clearly seen.

Giant's Causeway 1897 40429
From the late eighteenth century, the causeway was an important tourist attraction, and its popularity increased greatly when the Belfast to Portrush railway opened in 1883.

Giant's Causeway, The Wishing Chair 1897 40432
The Victorians gave fanciful names - such as the Wishing Chair to this 'basalt honeycomb'- to many of the natural features of the Causeway coast.

Portrush, The Harbour 1897 40401
Portrush harbour is situated on the west side of Ramore Head. In this view, steamers are moored along the quayside. There were once regular sailings to Glasgow and Greenock, but its days as a cross-channel port are now over.

**Portrush, Ladies'
Bathing Place 1897**
40399
A fine study of the
Ladies' Bathing Place,
which seems a popular
venue for both the
women and menfolk of
Portrush. A yacht can
be seen out towards the
Skerries.

Portrush, The Railway Station 1897 40409
The railway reached Portrush with the construction of a short branch line from Coleraine on the Belfast to
Londonderry line. The station was extensively remodelled in 1893, just four years before this picture was taken.
The electric railway to the Giant's Causeway started from outside the front of the station.

Portrush, Ladies' Bathing Place 1897 40398A
Another view of the pool, this time looking the other way, showing the rocky shore with the town in the
background.

Ardboe Cross, near Coagh c1950 C585301
The elaborate cross probably dates from the tenth century. It is richly carved with many scenes from the scriptures. It stands almost 20 ft tall and is a national monument.

Ballymoney, High Street c1900 B269001
This turn of the century view shows the broad and spacious high street. In the centre is the former town hall, later a masonic hall, which dates from 1775. With the exception of a curious bystander, the broad street is totally devoid of any traffic.

◀ **Lisburn, Market Square 1896** L138001
Although an old market town, Lisburn is at the heart of the Irish linen industry. Behind the market square can be seen the Protestant cathedral, built in 1623 and elevated to cathedral status in 1662.

◄ **Dromore, Market Day 1904** D79002
Market day is in full swing-carts are drawn up in the yard, and on the right farmers are huddled in conversation. A poster on the left advertises a Thanksgiving service.

▼ **Fintona, Main Street c1965** F189003
Looking down the street to the green hills of County Tyrone beyond. Note the kerbside petrol pumps on the right, a common Irish feature until recent times.

◄ **Fintona c1965** F189002
An evocative view of the town, showing remarkably little traffic or parked cars.

Monaghan, The Diamond c1870 M119001
An old picture of the original square and centre of the town known as the Diamond, which was the original market place of Monaghan. The market cross was moved a few years later to make way for the Rossmore Memorial.

Monaghan, The Diamond c1917 M119005
This picture of the Diamond now shows the elaborate neo-Gothic drinking fountain, the Rossmore Memorial, built in 1875 in honour of Baron Rossmore, a local dignitary.

Monaghan, Dawson Street c1910 M119002
A view looking south from Church Square along Dawson Street, which leads to Ballybay. The typical wide street is almost devoid of traffic, and the little boys posing for the camera can happily play in the street. The chimney is a reminder that the linen industry flourished here.

Monaghan, Old Cross Square 1900 M119004
This picture of the square at the south end of Dublin Street, is interesting in that it shows the original market cross, which was repositioned here when the Rossmore Memorial was erected in the Diamond in 1875.

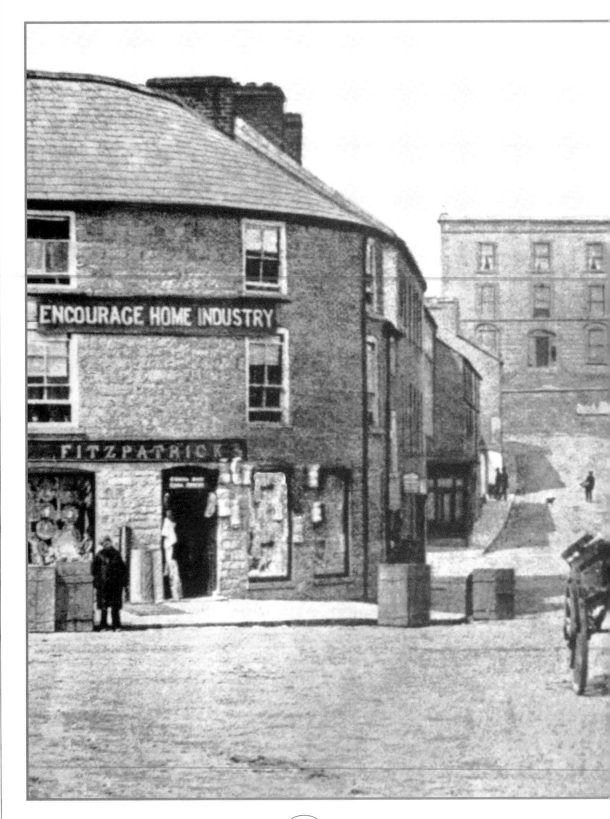

Monaghan, Mill Street c1900 M119006
An evocative view, with the shopkeepers and deliverymen posing for the photographer. Note the banner above Fitzpatrick's encouraging home industry.

Rossmore Castle c1900 M119003
An excellent view of the castle, the seat of the Rossmore family. This fine estate is about one and a half miles south of the town, on the minor road to Newbliss and Cavan. Little now remains, but the park is very popular.

Loughgall, Main Street c1960 L454002
A classic rural Irish scene of this period, a pleasing main street, devoid of any traffic save for a farmer chugging up the hill in his tractor.

Loughgall c1955 L454001
Loughgall is an attractive Armagh village on the minor road between Portadown and Armagh. This view shows a quiet scene with only a few motor cars.

Dublin

The capital of Ireland, the city of Dublin is beautifully situated in a bay at the mouth of the river Liffey. The Vikings established a defended ford and town here in the mid-ninth century, and today Dublin is an important port, as well as a cathedral and university city. Dublin is noted for its many gracious streets, including O'Connell Street, and its fine buildings, including the Four Courts, Customs House and the General Post Office. To the west of the city centre is the extensive Phoenix Park.

Dublin, Sackville Street 1897 39204
A view of O'Connell Street (then Sackville Street), looking north with the bridge over the Liffey in the foreground. The O'Connell and Nelson monuments are prominent. Horse-drawn trams are much in evidence.

Dublin, Sackville Street 1897 39205 Another view of Sackville Street, looking north to the Nelson Monument. This monument was badly damaged in 1966, and later demolished. Also prominent in the picture is the General Post Office, opened in 1818 and scene of the opening of the Easter rising in 1916.

Dublin, The O'Connell Monument 1897 39208
At the bottom of Sackville Street is the O'Connell Monument. Built in 1882, it was only fifteen years old at the time this picture was taken. The Nelson Monument is in the background.

Dublin, Sackville Street 1897 39206
A further view of Sackville Street, taken from the west side. Sackville (O'Connell) Street was, and is, one of Dublin's main thoroughfares. Even in 1897, it was busy with pedestrians, carts and horse-trams.

▼ **Dublin, Trinity College 1897** 39210
On the left of this view is Trinity College, which dates from 1759 and is 300 ft in length. On the right hand side is the Bank of Ireland, a building dating from Georgian times and once the home of the Irish Parliament.

▼ **Dublin, View along College Green 1897** 39212
A view looking east along the green to Trinity College, with the Bank of Ireland on the left. This bustling scene shows a horse-tram snaking over the cobbled street.

▲ **Dublin, Grafton Stree** **1897** 39215
This busy view looks north along Grafton Street, which links St Stephens' Green to the Liffey. In the foregrounc the road curves to the le round Trinity College. A horse-tram is heading into the city.

◀ **Dublin, The Four Courts 1897** 39224
This famous Dublin landmark is situated on the north bank of the Liffey, a little to the west of the centre. It was designed by James Gandon, and built between 1785-1802. Its most magnificent feature is the great dome. Like the Customs House, it was gutted by fire in the civil war, but was later restored.

Dublin, Christchurch Cathedral 1897 39254
Christchurch is the mother cathedral of the Church of Ireland. It is situated a short distance west of Trinity College. It dates back to 1030, but the current building dates from a thorough restoration between 1871 and 1878.

Dublin, Custom House 1897 39222
One of Dublin's most famous buildings is the Custom House. It was designed by Gandon and built between 1781-1791. It is situated on the north bank of the Liffey to the east of O'Connell Street, and was heavily damaged in the civil war, although restored a few years later. The railway line to Connolly station is visible just behind.

Dublin, The Castle 1897 39260
The present Dublin Castle is probably on the site of the original Viking fort guarding the crossing of the Liffey. At the time that this picture was taken, the castle was an important place of British administration. This view shows the state entrance.

Dublin, Phoenix Park 1897 39266
The park is a vast open space, 1,760 acres in area and seven miles around. The road across is straight for two miles. Near the Park Gate entrance at the city end stands the former Viceregal Lodge, once the home of the British Governor. It is now the President's palace.

**Dublin, The Harbour
1897** 39283
A further view of the
mouth of the River
Liffey, Dublin's harbour.
Dublin has always been
an important port,
particularly for goods
and merchandise. A
paddle steamer is
drawn up on the north
side, together with
other steamships.

Around Dublin

HOWTH

An important fishing port and suburb of Dublin, lying on the north of Dublin Bay beneath the 560 ft-high Howth Head. The artificial harbour was built in 1807-10 and was originally a packet station, but it silted up and the steamers moved to Dun Laoghaire. The harbour is protected from rough weather by the quartzite island, Ireland's Eye, which forms a natural breakwater, while the Baily Lighthouse, of 1814, stands on the site of an ancient fortress.

DUN LAOGHAIRE

Today a suburb of Dublin, Dun Laoghaire is situated eight miles to the south around Dublin Bay. Although the town and its satellites including Killiney, are seaside resorts, it is best known for its harbour and ferry service to Holyhead. At the time of these pictures, the town was known as Kingstown in honour of a visit by George IV in 1821. It reverted to its old name in the 1930s. The great harbour was built by John Rennie between 1817 and 1821.

Howth, Harbour Road 1897 39296
Looking east along the road, the view encompasses the ruined church and the little tower on the small promontory above the harbour. The only traffic is a small pony and trap.

POWERSCOURT

A large, old estate, situated about thirteen miles to the south of Dublin, and a few miles to the west of Bray.

The eighteenth-century house was once the seat of the Powerscourt family and probably stands on the site of an older castle. The gardens are especially beautiful, with views to the Sugar Loaf Mountain.

CLONMEL

A market town in the rolling Tipperary countryside, pleasantly situated on the river Suir with views south to the Comeragh Mountains. Founded in the thirteenth century, the town held out stoutly against Cromwell's forces. There are still traces of the former town walls. This rather fashionable town has many notable buildings, including the Church of St Mary.

Howth, Church of the Blessed Virgin Mary 1897 39287
The ruins of this collegiate parish church overlook Howth harbour. The church was founded in 1235 to take the place of St Nessan's on the nearby island of Ireland's Eye. The bells are preserved in Howth Castle.

Howth, The Harbour 1897 39292
A view of the spacious harbour, with assorted sailing craft. After the packet-boats moved to Dun Laoghaire, Howth settled down to life as a fishing harbour. The harbour was the scene of Nationalist gun-running in 1914.

Howth, Ireland's Eye 1897 39302
A final view looking around the sweeping east pier of Howth harbour to the lighthouse. In the distance, under a mile away, is Ireland's Eye, a small rocky island with an excellent beach and the ruins of the sixth century St Nessan's Abbey.

Kingstown, The Harbour 1897 39308
The harbour was begun in 1817, and ever since has been the principal terminus of the Holyhead run. The town was renamed Kingstown in 1821 in honour of a visit by George IV, but reverted to its former name of Dun Laoghaire after independence.

◄ **Kingstown, George IV Monument 1897** 39316
This view shows the monument which records the visit of George IV in 1821. It was damaged in the 1960s by the IRA. Behind is the Carlisle Pier, the former mail boat terminal, together with its station.

◄ Kingstown, The Harbour 1897 39311
A fine view of HMS Pelarus flying the white ensign, at anchor in Kingstown Harbour.

▼ Kingstown, Queen's Road 1897 39317
A view looking south along Queen's Road, the entrance to the pier is on the left. The church is a well-known landmark for those coming over in the ferry from Holyhead.

◄ Kingstown, The Town Hall and Railway Station 1897 39319
A superb view, taken from Royal Marine Road. The railway between Dublin and Kingstown was the first in Ireland, and was opened in 1834. Semaphore signals can be seen behind the bridge.

Kingstown, Killiney Head and Station 1897 39326
The line was opened through here in 1854, and there were originally stations at Killiney and Ballybrack. They were replaced by a combined station between the two in 1882. The old Killiney Station can be seen just beyond the footbridge.

Clonmel, Church of St Mary c1890 C684001
The church is a fine pre-Reformation church, now part of the Church of Ireland. St Mary's was heavily restored in the nineteenth century. It has a very unusual octagonal tower of massive proportions, as shown clearly in this picture.

Powerscourt, The Cascade 1890 24607
The River Dargle falls down a precipice of about 300 ft, and this has long been a popular spot with sightseers.

The South West

CORK

An important city, the third largest in Ireland, Cork is pleasantly situated on the River Lee. The origins of the city date back to the foundation of a monastery in the sixth century. It has survived attacks by Cromwell and William III, and is today a major seaport and industrial centre. There are many fine buildings and spacious streets, as well as Catholic and Protestant cathedrals.

SCHULL

A remote village in County Cork, it lies at the foot of the 1,339 ft Mount Gabriel, and looks southwards out over its harbour to the Atlantic Ocean and Clear Island. The scenery is wild and full of antiquities. The village was once connected to Skibbereen by a fascinating roadside tramway, which closed in 1947.

Cork, The Harbour 1898 C21901
A view of steamers moored on the River Lee at Cork Harbour. The Lee flows in two channels through Cork, which join up again near here to head out to sea. In those days, the Lee estuary saw many local paddle-steamer services between Cork, Blackrock and Cobh.

GLENGARRIFF

A little coastal resort at the head of Glengarriff Harbour, an inlet of Bantry Bay, which basks in a Mediterranean microclimate, thanks to the warm Gulf Stream and the orientation of the six-mile-long glen behind it, which is sheltered from north winds by mountains rising to over 2,000 ft. The name means 'rugged glen' in Irish, but its vegetation is luxuriant, with palms, fuchsias, hollies and arbutus among the mighty pine trees. Today Glengarriff is known for the gardens on Garinish, a little island in the harbour, which were laid out in the 1920s.

KILLARNEY

Famed worldwide as Ireland's most beautiful corner, Killarney has been the destination of tourists who delight in spectacular scenery since the eighteenth century.

At that time, the local landowner, Lord Kenmare, with remarkable foresight, founded the little town close to Lough Leane and offered incentives to hoteliers. The town throngs with holidaymakers, riding in 'jaunting cars' to view the lakes and the wild scenery of Ireland's highest mountains, Macgillycuddy's Reeks.

Cork, St Patrick's Street c1899 C21903
One of the more important streets in Cork, the spacious and curving street has many fine buildings. The only traffic is some carts.

Schull, The Pier c1955 S696003
A classic scene of the remote west of Ireland. At the entrance to the pier, a group of men stand passing the time of day, watching a group of small boys playing on the rowing boats drawn up on the foreshore. A dog waits patiently. In the background, the tiny village nestles under the slopes of Mount Gabriel.

Schull, The Pier c1955 S696001
A pleasing picture of the little pier at Schull. All is quiet, with rowing boats and a yacht moored in the small bay. Note the car at the entrance to the quayside.

◀ **Glengarriff, Eccles Hotel 1897** 40684
Glengarriff was a favourite tourist spot from the mid-nineteenth century when visited by Edward VII as Prince of Wales. The once-grand Eccles Hotel, facing the sea, attracted literary giants such as Thackeray, Yeats and Shaw. Its importance is summed up in the words of a nineteenth-century guide - that Glengarriff village is near the Eccles Hotel.

Schull, The Pier c1955 S696002

Another view of the pier, with a fishing boat drawn up against the harbour wall proving a source of interest for a little group of bystanders. The wide sweep of the bay provides shelter for the fishing boats.

Glengarriff, The Post Office 1897 40687

The tall trees and luxuriant vegetation of Glengarriff are apparent in this view. Glengarriff was a very popular resort with well-off Victorians, who followed the 'Prince of Wales' route from Cork to Bantry and from thence by steamer to Glengarriff before travelling on by mail car to Kenmare and Killarney.

Glengarriff, Police Barracks 1897 40688

The Victorians love of creeper-clad buildings is shown admirably in this view of the Glengarriff Police Barracks.

Glengarriff, The Harbour 1897 40706
A peaceful view showing Otter Rock and Brandy island, taken on a still day, with the boats' reflections hardly stirring in the water.

Killarney, Kenmare House 1897 40631
An evocative view of this Victorian Tudor mansion, destroyed by fire prior to World War I. It is shown here in its former splendour, with its famous gardens that sloped down to Lough Leane.

Innisfallen, Landing Place 1898 40620

A magical picture of the landing place on Innisfallen, a 21-acre island in Lough Leane near Killarney. Behind the rowing boat and the landing stage, sheep can be seen grazing amidst the ruins of the abbey, which was founded in the seventh century.

Innisfallen, The Oratory 1897 40623

A view of the most impressive part of the remains of the abbey, the tiny oratory, with its Irish-Romanesque west doorway. The Annals of Innisfallen, written by the monks here, is an important early history of Ireland.

Killarney, Old Weir Bridge 1897 40643
This old weir, where the river rushes through the gap, is near the end of the Long Range, and close to 'The meeting of the waters'. Here, a man in a rowing boat is surveying the weir.

▼ **Killarney, Ross Castle 1897** 40639
The castle, situated about one and a half miles south of Killarney, is close to the shore of Lough Leane. The keep dates from the fourteenth century and was surrendered by Lord Muskerry to Cromwell's troops in 1652.

▼ **Killarney, Long Range 1897** 40646
A view of the end of the Long Range, the beautiful narrow lake between Lough Leane and the Upper Lake, which lies under the shadow of Eagle's Nest, a precipitous mountain 1,100 ft high.

▲ **Killarney, 'The Meeting of the Waters** **1897** 40647
After Old Weir Bridge th stream divides at 'The meeting of the waters'. The west channel heads round Dinish island whil the east heads into Muckross Lake. In the foreground are a group sightseers.

◄ **Killarney, Muckross Lake 1897** 40654
This view further to the east shows the Muckross Lake (Middle Lake). In the background is the 1,764 ft-high Torc Mountain, which dominates the lake here. A party of rowers is on the little landing stage.

Killarney, Macgillycuddy's Reeks 1897 40660
A classic Killarney view looking up to the massive Macgillycuddy's Reeks. A rowing boat is drawn up in the foreground, and a group of people linger by the edge of the lake.

Killarney, Road Tunnel 1897 40673
A photograph of the well-known landmark of Killarney, the road tunnel on the Killarney to Kenmare road. The tunnel is beneath Cromaglan mountain, near the shore of the Upper Lake.

Killarney, Kate Kearney's Cottage c1955 K19003
The road through the Gap of Dunloe is probably the best-known attraction of Killarney, and starts from the old alehouse, once kept by the infamous Kate Kearney and now named after her.

Killarney, The Gap of Dunloe Road c1955 K19004
The trip along the four-mile minor road over the Gap is spectacular, with the road crossing and re-crossing the river at the bottom of the ravine. In this view, the road is climbing to Black Lake, where it can be seen crossing the river.

◀ **Muckross Abbey 1897**
40608
Another view, this time showing a close-up of the abbey church, revealing the square tower and the four light east window. The abbey was sacked in Cromwell's time and has been ruinous ever since.

Muckross Abbey 1897

40609

Approximately three miles south of Killarney is Muckross Abbey. It was founded by the Franciscans in 1440, but the site is much older. This view shows extensive ruins covered in ivy, and an unkempt graveyard.

Muckross Abbey c1955

K19008

In the fifty eight years from the picture opposite (40609), the ruins and graveyard have been cleaned up, and the ivy removed. The surrounding countryside of the Muckross Desmesne is noted for its beauty.

Killarney, Brickeen Bridge c1955 K19014

Muckross Lake and Lough Leane are separated by Muckross Desmesne and Dinish Island. The island and the Desmesne are connected by Brickeen Bridge, a handsome stone bridge with a pointed arch.

The West

GALWAY

The city stands at an ancient site where the River Corrib foams into Galway Bay. Galway was fortified before the Anglo-Norman de Burgo family built their castle here in the 1230s, and it remained a walled town until the seventeenth century. Christopher Columbus is said to have worshipped at St Nicholas' church when he visited Ireland researching the voyages of St Brendan. The modern cathedral dates from 1965.

SPIDDAL

A small village situated on the north side of Galway Bay. Today it is a small resort, well-known for its sandy beach, which looks south across the bay to County Clare and the fascinating Burren Region. Spiddal is also the gateway into Connemara and the Gaelic-speaking area.

Galway, Salmon Weir Bridge c1955 G273006
Looking across the River Corrib at Salmon Weir bridge, built in 1818 to link the new courthouse (1815) and the old jail, whose site is now occupied by the new cathedral.

HEADFORD

Lying north of Galway and just to the east of Lough Corrib, Headford has served for many years as a local market centre. It is known today for the picturesque ruins of the Franciscan Ross Friary of 1351, just to the north west off the Cong road.

CONNEMARA

Connemara is one of the wildest and most beautiful regions of Ireland. It starts west of Galway, and Clifden, a tiny town about fifty miles away on the Atlantic coast, is its centre. Connemara is dominated by The Twelve Bens, the highest of which is almost 2,400 ft. The rugged coastline is broken by small islands, and tiny harbours and villages abound, perhaps the finest being at Roundstone. It is a Gaelic-speaking area, and is popular with tourists, hikers and anglers.

MAYO

A little-known county on the north-western seaboard of Ireland, it nevertheless has some of Ireland's most famous attractions. Westport is a fine town, close to Croagh Patrick, Ireland's 'Holy Mountain'. Off Clew Bay is Achill Island, with its 2,000 ft-high cliffs. Inland, there are many beautiful mountains and lakes.

ACHILL ISLAND

The largest island off the Irish coast, it is separated from Mayo by a narrow tidal sound. Achill is a rugged mountainous island, with fine cliff scenery and beaches.

The land is poor and until recently the menfolk of the island used to leave in spring to work on farms in Scotland, saving enough to see them through the difficult winter. A stronghold of the Irish language antiquities, it is today a popular tourist location.

Galway, Salmon Weir c1955 G273002
The white waters of the River Corrib foam through the weir. Salmon still mass below the weirs in spring and the town's former mills have found a new life as apartment blocks.

Galway, The Beach c1955 G273003
A view of one of the beaches which look out over Galway Bay to County Clare and the limestone landscape of the Burren.

Spiddal, The Beach c1965 S663001
The beach at Spiddal has always been popular with Galway folk and other tourists. In this scene, the beach is quiet, with bathers enjoying a summer swim. The village is in the distance.

▼ **Headford, Market Day c1955** H435001
A vanished Irish scene: crates of fine young pigs for sale on a sunny market day in Headford.

▼ **Connemara, View of Lough Ballynakill c1955** C586003
A view looking eastwards along the rocky Barnaderg Bay towards Letterfrack and Diamond Hill. Letterfrack, situated in the heart of the National Park, is one of the major centres of Connemara.

▲ **Connemara, Roundstone Harbour c1955** C586014
The many bays and inlets of Connemara are dotted with little harbours and villages. One of the largest is Roundstone, situated on the coast road between Recess and Clifden. This view shows the picturesque harbour, looking east to the other side of the bay.

◄ Connemara, View of Barnaderg Bay c.1955

C586016

Barnaderg bay at the end of Ballynakill Harbour, close to Letterfrack. In the distance is the mountainous tract of Connemara. A rather beautiful boat is drawn up on the rocky foreshore.

A Connemara 'Boreen' c1955 C586004
A classic view of a 'boreen' or small road. The luxuriant vegetation reveals the almost Mediterranean climate of the west coast, whilst the roads hereabouts are dotted with isolated smallholdings.

Mayo, Doo Lough c1955 D203001
A charming view of picturesque Doo Lough, situated in the wild mountain scenery on the road north from Connemara to Louisberg. The mountain on the left is the Mweelrea, reaching over 2,000 ft in height.

Mayo, Croagh Patrick c1955 C587002
A view taken along the coast road between Westport and Louisberg, showing the almost conical Croagh Patrick. Situated about six miles south-west of Westport, it rises just over 2,500 ft from the south shore of Clew Bay.

Mayo, Lough Cloon c1965 L453001
A marvellously peaceful view of Lough Cloon, about eight miles north of Ballinrobe, one of the many lakes in this part of Mayo, of which the largest is Lough Mask. This area, known as Joyce's Country, is to the east of Connemara and is dominated by the Partry Mountains.

◄ **Achill Island, Dooagh Village c1955** A311009
A view of this remote village, the largest settlement on Achill. Behind is Croaghaun, almost 2,200 ft high, which on the far side drops precipitously to the Atlantic.

◀ **Quayside, Achill c1955** A311004
A peaceful scene looking towards the 2,204 ft high Slievemore. Achill is separated from the Mayo coast by a narrow strait, crossed by a swing bridge built in 1888. The railway once ran from Westport to Achill village, but closed in 1937.

▼ **Achill Island, Dooagh Village c1955** A311010
This magnificent view shows a typical Achill scene, clouds hanging over Croaghaun, whilst the limewashed cottages huddle together in this remote Irish-speaking village.

◀ **Dooagh, Thatched Cottage c1955** A311013
Another scene typical of western Ireland: thatched cottage, hens scratching for food and an island woman with her shawl. Next door is another familiar scene, a derelict cottage, reflecting the flight of many of the population from the constant struggle for survival.

Achill Island, Dooega, The Village c1955 A311002
A nostalgic scene of tiny Dooega, a cluster of cottages on the south western seaboard of Achill. Fishing nets are left out to dry on the cobbles at the top of the beach.

Achill Island, Dooega, View Across across Camport Bay c1955 A311014
A marvellous view looking west from an old farmstead across the bay to the village. In the distance, clouds are enveloping the Menawn. On the left, turf is stacked drying in the sun for the winter.

Index

Frith Book Co Titles

Frith Book Company publish over a 100 new titles each year. For latest catalogue please contact Frith Book Co.

Town Books 96pp, 100 photos. County and Themed Books 128pp, 150 photos (unless specified) All titles hardback laminated case and jacket except those indicated pb (paperback)

Around Barnstaple	1-85937-084-5	£12.99
Around Blackpool	1-85937-049-7	£12.99
Around Bognor Regis	1-85937-055-1	£12.99
Around Bristol	1-85937-050-0	£12.99
Around Cambridge	1-85937-092-6	£12.99
Cheshire	1-85937-045-4	£14.99
Around Chester	1-85937-090-X	£12.99
Around Chesterfield	1-85937-071-3	£12.99
Around Chichester	1-85937-089-6	£12.99
Cornwall	1-85937-054-3	£14.99
Cotswolds	1-85937-099-3	£14.99
Around Derby	1-85937-046-2	£12.99
Devon	1-85937-052-7	£14.99
Dorset	1-85937-075-6	£14.99
Dorset Coast	1-85937-062-4	£14.99
Around Dublin	1-85937-058-6	£12.99
East Anglia	1-85937-059-4	£14.99
Around Eastbourne	1-85937-061-6	£12.99
English Castles	1-85937-078-0	£14.99
Around Falmouth	1-85937-066-7	£12.99
Hampshire	1-85937-064-0	£14.99
Isle of Man	1-85937-065-9	£14.99
Around Maidstone	1-85937-056-X	£12.99
North Yorkshire	1-85937-048-9	£14.99
Around Nottingham	1-85937-060-8	£12.99
Around Penzance	1-85937-069-1	£12.99
Around Reading	1-85937-087-X	£12.99
Around St Ives	1-85937-068-3	£12.99
Around Salisbury	1-85937-091-8	£12.99
Around Scarborough	1-85937-104-3	£12.99
Scottish Castles	1-85937-077-2	£14.99
Around Sevenoaks and Tonbridge	1-85937-057-8	£12.99

Sheffield and S Yorkshire	1-85937-070-5	£14.99
Shropshire	1-85937-083-7	£14.99
Staffordshire	1-85937-047-0 (96pp)	£12.99
Suffolk	1-85937-074-8	£14.99
Surrey	1-85937-081-0	£14.99
Around Torbay	1-85937-063-2	£12.99
Wiltshire	1-85937-053-5	£14.99
Around Bakewell	1-85937-113-2	£12.99
Around Bournemouth	1-85937-067-5	£12.99
Cambridgeshire	1-85937-086-1	£14.99
Essex	1-85937-082-9	£14.99
Around Great Yarmouth	1-85937-085-3	£12.99
Hertfordshire	1-85937-079-9	£14.99
Isle of Wight	1-85937-114-0	£14.99
Around Lincoln	1-85937-111-6	£12.99
Oxfordshire	1-85937-076-4	£14.99
Around Shrewsbury	1-85937-110-8	£12.99
South Devon Coast	1-85937-107-8	£14.99
Around Stratford upon Avon	1-85937-098-5	£12.99
West Midlands	1-85937-109-4	£14.99

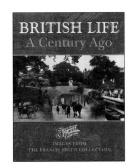

British Life A Century Ago
246 x 189mm
144pp, hardback.
Black and white
Lavishly illustrated with photos from the turn of the century, and with extensive commentary. It offers a unique insight into the social history and heritage of bygone Britain.

1-85937-103-5 £17.99

Available from your local bookshop or from the publisher

Frith Book Co Titles Available in 2000

Around Bath	1-85937-097-7	£12.99	Mar
County Durham	1-85937-123-x	£14.99	Mar
Cumbria	1-85937-101-9	£14.99	Mar
Down the Thames	1-85937-121-3	£14.99	Mar
Around Exeter	1-85937-126-4	£12.99	Mar
Greater Manchester	1-85937-108-6	£14.99	Mar
Around Guildford	1-85937-117-5	£12.99	Mar
Around Harrogate	1-85937-112-4	£12.99	Mar
Around Leicester	1-85937-073-x	£12.99	Mar
Around Liverpool	1-85937-051-9	£12.99	Mar
Around Newark	1-85937-105-1	£12.99	Mar
Northumberland and Tyne & Wear			
	1-85937-072-1	£14.99	Mar
Around Oxford	1-85937-096-9	£12.99	Mar
Around Plymouth	1-85937-119-1	£12.99	Mar
Around Southport	1-85937-106-x	£12.99	Mar
Welsh Castles	1-85937-120-5	£14.99	Mar
Around Belfast	1-85937-094-2	£12.99	Apr
Canals and Waterways	1-85937-129-9	£17.99	Apr
Down the Severn	1-85937-118-3	£14.99	Apr
East Sussex	1-85937-130-2	£14.99	Apr
Exmoor	1-85937-132-9	£14.99	Apr
Gloucestershire	1-85937-102-7	£14.99	Apr
Around Horsham	1-85937-127-2	£12.99	Apr
Around Ipswich	1-85937-133-7	£12.99	Apr
Ireland (pb)	1-85937-181-7	£9.99	Apr
Kent Living Memories	1-85937-125-6	£14.99	Apr
London (pb)	1-85937-183-3	£9.99	Apr
New Forest	1-85937-128-0	£14.99	Apr
Scotland (pb)	1-85937-182-5	£9.99	Apr
Around Southampton	1-85937-088-8	£12.99	Apr
Stone Circles & Ancient Monuments			
	1-85937-143-4	£17.99	Apr
Sussex (pb)	1-85937-184-1	£9.99	Apr
Colchester (pb)	1-85937-188-4	£8.99	May
County Maps of Britain			
	1-85937-156-6 (192pp)	£19.99	May
Leicestershire (pb)	1-85937-185-x	£9.99	May

Lincolnshire	1-85937-135-3	£14.99	May
Around Newquay	1-85937-140-x	£12.99	May
Nottinghamshire (pb)	1-85937-187-6	£9.99	May
Redhill to Reigate	1-85937-137-x	£12.99	May
Victorian & Edwardian Yorkshire			
	1-85937-154-x	£14.99	May
Around Winchester	1-85937-139-6	£12.99	May
Yorkshire (pb)	1-85937-186-8	£9.99	May
Berkshire (pb)	1-85937-191-4	£9.99	Jun
Brighton (pb)	1-85937-192-2	£8.99	Jun
Dartmoor	1-85937-145-0	£14.99	Jun
East London	1-85937-080-2	£14.99	Jun
Glasgow (pb)	1-85937-190-6	£8.99	Jun
Kent (pb)	1-85937-189-2	£9.99	Jun
Victorian & Edwardian Kent			
	1-85937-149-3	£14.99	Jun
North Devon Coast	1-85937-146-9	£14.99	Jun
Peak District	1-85937-100-0	£14.99	Jun
Around Truro	1-85937-147-7	£12.99	Jun
Victorian & Edwardian Maritime Album			
	1-85937-144-2	£17.99	Jun
West Sussex	1-85937-148-5	£14.99	Jun
Churches of Berkshire	1-85937-170-1	£17.99	Jul
Churches of Dorset	1-85937-172-8	£17.99	Jul
Churches of Hampshire	1-85937-207-4	£17.99	Jul
Churches of Wiltshire	1-85937-171-x	£17.99	Jul
Derbyshire (pb)	1-85937-196-5	£9.99	Jul
Edinburgh (pb)	1-85937-193-0	£8.99	Jul
Herefordshire	1-85937-174-4	£14.99	Jul
Norwich (pb)	1-85937-194-9	£8.99	Jul
Ports and Harbours	1-85937-208-2	£17.99	Jul
Somerset and Avon	1-85937-153-1	£14.99	Jul
South Devon Living Memories			
	1-85937-168-x	£14.99	Jul
Warwickshire (pb)	1-85937-203-1	£9.99	Jul
Worcestershire	1-85937-152-3	£14.99	Jul
Yorkshire Living Memories			
	1-85937-166-3	£14.99	Jul

FRITH PRODUCTS & SERVICES

Francis Frith would doubtless be pleased to know that the pioneering publishing venture he started in 1860 still continues today. More than a hundred and thirty years later, The Francis Frith Collection continues in the same innovative tradition and is now one of the foremost publishers of vintage photographs in the world. Some of the current activities include:

Interior Decoration

Today Frith's photographs can be seen framed and as giant wall murals in thousands of pubs, restaurants, hotels, banks, retail stores and other public buildings throughout the country. In every case they enhance the unique local atmosphere of the places they depict and provide reminders of gentler days in an increasingly busy and frenetic world.

Product Promotions

Frith products have been used by many major companies to promote the sales of their own products or to reinforce their own history and heritage. Brands include Hovis bread, Courage beers, Scots Porage Oats, Colman's mustard, Cadbury's foods, Mellow Birds coffee, Dunhill pipe tobacco, Guinness, and Bulmer's Cider.

Genealogy and Family History

As the interest in family history and roots grows world-wide, more and more people are turning to Frith's photographs of Great Britain for images of the towns, villages and streets where their ancestors lived; and, of course, photographs of the churches and chapels where their ancestors were christened, married and buried are an essential part of every genealogy tree and family album.

A series of easy-to-use CD Roms is planned for publication, and an increasing number of Frith photographs will be able to be viewed on specialist genealogy sites. A growing range of Frith books will be available on CD.

The Internet

Already thousands of Frith photographs can be viewed and purchased on the internet. By the end of the year 2000 some 60,000 Frith photographs will be available on the internet. The number of sites is constantly expanding, each focussing on different products and services from the Collection.

Some of the sites are listed below.

www.townpages.co.uk
www.icollector.com
www.barclaysquare.co.uk
www.cornwall-online.co.uk

For background information on the Collection look at the three following sites:

www.francisfrith.com
www.francisfrith.co.uk
www.frithbook.co.uk

Frith Products

All Frith photographs are available Framed or just as Mounted Prints, and can be ordered from the address below. From time to time other products - Address Books, Calendars, Table Mats, etc - are available.

For further information:
if you would like further information on any of the above aspects of the Frith business please contact us at the address below:
The Francis Frith Collection,
Frith's Barn, Teffont, Salisbury, Wiltshire,
England SP3 5QP.
Tel: +44 (0)1722 716 376 Fax: +44 (0)1722 716 881   Email: uksales@francisfrith.com

---

To receive your FREE Mounted Print

Mounted Print
Overall size 14 x 11 inches

Cut out this Voucher and return it with your remittance for £1.50 to cover postage and handling. Choose any photograph included in this book. Your SEPIA print will be A4 in size, and mounted in a cream mount with burgundy rule lines, overall size 14 x 11 inches.

Order additional Mounted Prints at HALF PRICE (only £7.49 each*)

If there are further pictures you would like to order, possibly as gifts for friends and family, acquire them at half price (no additional postage and handling required).

Have your Mounted Prints framed*

For an additional £14.95 per print you can have your chosen Mounted Print framed in an elegant polished wood and gilt moulding, overall size 16 x 13 inches (no additional postage and handling required).

---

* IMPORTANT!
These special prices are only available if ordered using the original voucher on this page (no copies permitted) and at the same time as your free Mounted Print, for delivery to the same address

---

Frith Collectors' Guild

From time to time we publish a magazine of news and stories about Frith photographs and further special offers of Frith products. If you would like 12 months FREE membership, please return this form.

Send completed forms to:

The Francis Frith Collection, Frith's Barn, Teffont, Salisbury, Wiltshire SP3 5QP

Voucher for FREE and Reduced Price Frith Prints

Picture no.	Page number	Qty	Mounted @ £7.49	Framed + £14.95	Total Cost
		1	Free of charge*	£	£
			£7.49	£	£
			£7.49	£	£
			£7.49	£	£
			£7.49	£	£
			£7.49	£	£
			* Post & handling		£1.50

Book Title . . . .   **Total Order Cost**   £

Please do not photocopy this voucher. Only the original is valid, so please cut it out and return it to us.

I enclose a cheque / postal order for £ . . . .
made payable to 'The Francis Frith Collection'
OR please debit my Mastercard / Visa / Switch / Amex card

Number . . . .

Expires . . . . Signature . . . .

Name Mr/Mrs/Ms . . . .

Address . . . .

. . . .

. . . .

. . . .

. . . . Postcode . . . .

Daytime Tel No . . . .   Valid to 31/12/01

The Francis Frith Collectors' Guild

Please enrol me as a member for 12 months free of charge.

Name Mr/Mrs/Ms . . . .

Address . . . .

. . . .

. . . .

. . . . Postcode . . . .